Published by Creative Education
123 South Broad Street, Mankato, Minnesota 56001
Creative Education is an imprint of The Creative Company

Designed by Stephanie Blumenthal
Production Design by Tamarin Graphics

Photographs by Thomas R. Fletcher, Beryl Goldberg, Galyn C. Hammond,
Erwin C. "Bud" Nielsen, Ardella Reed, Root Resources, Anthony Russo,
Eugene G. Schulz, Tom Stack & Associates, Tom Till, Visuals Unlimited

Library of Congress Cataloging-in-Publication Data

Richardson, Adele, 1966–
Israel / by Adele Richardson
p. cm. — (Let's Investigate)
Includes glossary and index
Summary: Examines the history, landscape, wildlife, people, and
weather of the nation of Israel.
ISBN 1-58341-033-3
1. Israel—Juvenile literature. [1. Israel.] I. Title.
II. Series: Let's Investigate (Mankato, Minn.)
DS118.R486   2000
956.94—dc21   99-30514

First edition

2 4 6 8 9 7 5 3 1

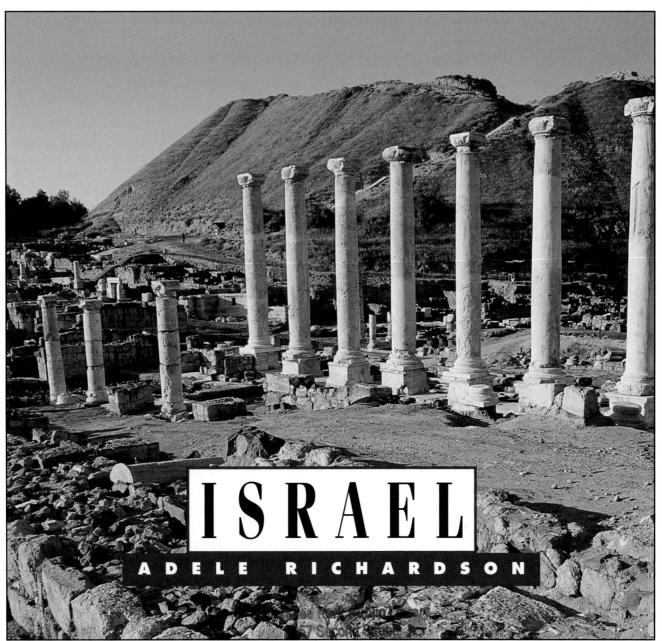

ISRAEL

ADELE RICHARDSON

Palisades Park, NJ 07650

Creative Education

ISREAL

ISRAEL

SIZE

Nearly six million people live in Israel, a country with about the same amount of land as the state of New Jersey.

Right, Timna Cliffs and rock formations in Timna National Park, which is located in Israel's Great Rift Valley near the Red Sea Below, red-eyed bulbul

Israel's official name is the State of Israel. It became one of the youngest countries in the world after forming in 1948. Over the next 50 years, the country would see many wars as its land was fought over. Despite this, it is the national homeland for people of the Jewish faith, a place of safety and comfort. Israel welcomes people of many religions to come and make it their home. A land of beauty and wonder, Israel is like no other place on Earth.

ISRAEL
RIVER

The Jordan River, Israel's longest river, flows for only about 199 miles (320 km).

Mosaic tile walls of the Dome of the Rock

A SMALL COUNTRY

Israel is a small, narrow country located in the southwestern part of Asia known as the Middle East. It stretches 290 miles (470 km) from north to south and only 85 miles (135 km) from east to west. It has many borders.

Neighboring countries are Syria, Jordan, Lebanon, and Egypt; the Mediterranean Sea touches part of Israel's east coast. This nation is unique because its land is the meeting place for three continents: Europe, Asia, and Africa. Israel's landscape varies greatly: the coastal plain is a strip of farmland that runs along the Mediterranean Sea, while some of the beaches in the northern part of the country have cliffs made of chalk and sandstone that drop straight down into the sea.

ISRAEL
RAIN

Three-fourths of the rain that Israel receives all year long falls entirely during December.

Above, three ancient buildings: Mariamne Tower, the Citadel, and David's Tower

ISRAEL

TRAVEL

8

Above, ancient Roman aqueduct used to transport water

The Golan Heights in the northeast is a range of mountains that were originally formed from old erupting volcanoes. Included in this area are the hills of Galilee. They range in height from 1,600 to 4,000 feet (500 to 1,200 m) above sea level. The Negev Desert takes up the land in the southern half of the country. Farther south, the country becomes more dry and desert-like.

Much of the Negev is filled with dry **gorges**, colorful sandstone, and rocky plateaus. It can be very dangerous in winter when rain causes sudden flooding and fills dry riverbeds called *wadis*.

Running down the entire length of the eastern part of the country is the Jordan Rift Valley and the Arava. Here the Jordan River flows south into the Dead Sea. The Arava is the desert **savannah** forming the nation's border south of the Dead Sea.

ISRAEL
FLAG

On Israel's flag is the design of a Jewish prayer shawl and blue Star of David, an important Jewish religious symbol.

Left, shepherd tending a flock of sheep along the Jericho Road
Below, the Israeli flag

ISRAEL

HISTORY

Most of the land described in the Bible is found within Israel's borders.

**Above, helmutted gecko
Right, poppy field
Opposite, mustard
blooming in the foothills
of Mount Tabor**

THE CLIMATE

Much of Israel has hot, dry summers and cool winters. From May to October the country has constant sunshine during the day and hardly any rainfall. The rainy season is November through April, with December being the wettest month. Most rain, however, falls in the northern half of the country, though it does sometimes rain in the desert region. The hottest month of the year is August.

ISRAEL
SEA

Above, ancient ruins uncovered in Jerusalem Right, a minaret, or tower, overlooking the Mediterranean Sea in Jaffa, Israel

Israel's temperatures vary, depending on the landscape. In the north, where there are hills and mountains, an average summer temperature may be around 95°F (35°C). However, near the Dead Sea and in the desert, summer temperatures can soar to 120°F (49°C).

Winters are usually mild, with temperatures ranging from 40° to 50°F (4° to 10°C). Sometimes snow falls in the hills and mountains. On a very rare occasion, the city of Jerusalem experiences snowfall.

A traveler can drive a car completely across Israel, from north to south, in about nine hours.

Left, leopard
Below, hooded vulture

PLANTS AND ANIMALS

Since Israel is touched by three different continents, it is home to a wide variety of plant and animal life. In fact, more than 2,800 different types of plants have been identified within the country. Some, such as the papyrus reed, cannot grow any further north than Israel's borders.

ISRAEL
M O O N

*Jewish and **Muslim** calendars are based on the movement of the moon, so major holidays rarely fall on the same date from year to year.*

Above, hyrax
Right, Nubian ibex

Many birds, ranging in size from tiny singing warblers to huge eagles and vultures, fly through Israel's skies. More than 380 different kinds of birds make Israel their home. Some of the birds live year round in the country. Others only pass through while they **migrate** north or south twice a year.

Israel's other animal life is also varied. Mountain and hilly areas are the **habitat** of gazelles. Foxes and leopards can be found in wooded areas. The desert is where the sure-footed ibex, a type of goat, leaps from rock to rock. Living all over the country are more than 80 species of reptiles, including snakes and lizards, as well as 135 different kinds of colorful butterflies.

Many animals in Israel are protected by laws. Over 1,545 square miles (4,000 sq km) of the country's land have been set aside as nature preserves. This means the land is left alone for wildlife to live without human interference. Israel has about 280 of these protected areas.

ISRAEL
SIGNS

Because so many different people live and travel through Israel, many of the road and street signs there are written in the Arabic, Hebrew, and English languages.

Left, ruins of the ancient Roman port city of Caesarea, located on the coast of Israel Below, street signs in Israel are printed in three languages

בית שאן
بيسان
BET SHE'AN

רמאלה
رام الله
RAMALLAH

ISRAEL
WORD

The Jewish word shalom *has three different meanings: peace, hello, and goodbye.*

The traditional Israeli dress for women includes a veil over the head and face

CITIES AND RURAL COMMUNITIES

Since the time Israel was founded, the population has grown 700 percent. Nine out of every ten Israeli people live in a city. Like other cities around the world, Jerusalem is filled with clogged roads, tall office buildings, and many museums and universities. Most people in the city live in high-rise apartment buildings. There are very few individual houses.

Almost all Israeli children attend school, which is free until a child reaches 18 years of age.

Most students start out in a nursery school, then go on to kindergarten. Students then attend six years of elementary school, three years of junior high school, and three more years of high school. Since education is so important, most young people go on to study at a college or university.

All that education is necessary because many jobs in Israeli cities involve working with lasers, computers, or chemicals; scientific and medical research are also important fields.

ISRAEL
LIFE

Even though the Negev Desert takes up half of Israel's land, only eight percent of the Israeli population lives in that area.

ISRAEL
SOLAR

All new homes built in Israel are now required by law to have solar-powered water heaters instead of gas or electric ones.

An area of Jerusalem known as the "Jewish Quarter"

ISRAEL
DIAMONDS

Diamonds are mined, or dug, from the earth in Israel. At the end of the 20th century, eight out of ten diamonds used in the world were discovered in Israel.

Above, stained glass window in a church Right, ruins of the Old City of Jerusalem, now a park and museum

People may also choose jobs in the field of **tourism**, such as working at hotels, becoming tour guides, or working to promote tourism.

Jerusalem, with nearly 600,000 people, is Israel's largest city. Tourists come from all over the world for the unique experience that only Israel can provide.

ISRAEL

Israeli law states that all men must join the army at age 18 and stay until they are 21; many men choose to stay in the army longer.

Left, Bet She'an, a site of excavation, or digging Below, veiled chameleon

ISRAEL

Above, fallow deer Center, Church of the Holy Sepulchre in the Old City of Jerusalem

In addition, Jerusalem has been the national and spiritual center for people of Jewish faith for about 3,000 years. Outside Jerusalem and Israel's other large cities, many **rural** people live in small villages made up of Arab and Druze cultures. Each village is a collective community, called a *kibbutz*. In the kibbutz everything is shared equally among the people, including land, money, homes, childcare, and food. Many people in a kibbutz are farmers, but some are also involved in fields of industry and tourism.

ISRAEL

SYMBOL

The official symbol of the nation of Israel is the menorah, a traditional candle holder with seven branches.

Above, menorah collection

The Sea of Galilee is technically a lake. At 696 feet (212 m) below sea level, it is the lowest freshwater lake on Earth.

Above, papyrus reeds
Right, Ein Gedi Spring
in Nahal David Nature
Reserve

Another type of rural community is the *moshav*. In this kind of settlement, the village people own their land and live independent lives where not everything is shared. However, like the kibbutz, many members are farmers and sell their crops as a group. New members can join a moshav only if the whole village agrees.

Many different kinds of food are eaten in Israel. Some are traditional Jewish dishes, such as chicken soup and chopped liver. Many restaurants and hotels serve **kosher** meals; others are fast food restaurants that serve the same fast foods found in North America.

Many fresh fruits and vegetables, as well as all kinds of breads, are found on Israel's dinner tables. One of the most popular snack foods is *falafel*.

ISRAEL
LETTERS

The Hebrew alphabet is written from right to left. All of its 22 letters are consonants; vowels are indicated by special marks above or below each letter.

ISRAEL
TREES

Since 1948, more than 200 million trees have been planted in Israel to help protect the soil from **erosion**.

Many types of plants are grown in experimental greenhouses in Israel

23

ISRAEL

FARMS

Many farmers do not use water sprinklers to **irrigate** *crops; instead they use a system of tubes that drip water.*

Above, red peppers boxed for sale Citrus pomelos (top), safflower (bottom), and Japanese melons (opposite) are important Israeli crops

Falafel is soft, flat pita bread filled with pickles, sauce, and fried chickpeas. It is such a favorite snack that vendors sell it at stands in all Israeli cities. The country is able to grow nearly all the food its people eat. This is very surprising, considering more than half of the tiny country is rocky and dry—not the best conditions for farming. Despite this, many farms exist all over Israel.

Melons, citrus fruits, tomatoes, and peppers, as well as a wide assortment of flowers, grow all year round.

ISRAEL
F A C T

The National Water Carrier was built in 1964. Builders took 10 years to complete the 4,037-mile-long (6,500 km) pipeline.

Right, many of the buildings in the Old City of Jerusalem are linked with stone-covered passageways Above, St. George's Monastery

The most amazing thing is that these foods are grown in an unlikely place: the desert.

Farming in the desert is possible due to the National Water Carrier. It is a vast network of pumping stations, pipes, and canals that bring fresh water from the north to the dry south. Since so little rain falls, many farmers rely on the Water Carrier to irrigate their fields.

Israel is a very religious country. In fact, it is often called the Holy Land because it is the birthplace of three major religions: **Judaism**, **Islam**, and **Christianity**. Israel promises religious freedom to every person. This means that it doesn't matter what religion people believe in.

All believers are able to observe their religion's laws and holidays within Israel's borders. Eight out of every ten people in Israel belong to the Jewish faith. Many Jewish believers go to the Western Wall in Jerusalem to say their prayers. This place is called the Wailing Wall. Other Jewish followers practice their religion in places called synagogues, which are buildings similar to churches.

ISRAEL
F A C T

The religious day of rest for followers of Islam is Friday, while Jews observe Saturday, and Christians observe Sunday. The Israeli government recognizes all of these days as special.

27

The Dome of the Rock

ISRAEL

An ancient Jewish law requires farmers to not plant crops in their fields every seventh year.

ISRAEL

The Neot Kedumin is a preserve for plants in Israel. The workers there collect and raise species of plants that are mentioned in the Bible.

Sandstone arches in Timna National Park

Near the Western Wall is the Dome of the Rock. Like many Israeli buildings, it is covered with mosaic tiles, colorful pieces arranged in patterns. It was built as a **monument** to the Islamic prophet Muhammad. On Fridays, the day of rest, the followers of Islam (called Muslims) pray at the El Aqsa Mosque in Jerusalem.

ISRAEL
RIVER

As the Jordan River flows south from Mount Hermon, it gradually drops near-ly 2,300 feet (701 m) before emptying into the Dead Sea.

The Arabian oryx is an endangered animal

ISRAEL

BOOKS

Despite the small size of Israel, this nation has more than 750 public libraries.

ISRAEL

SWEET

The Jewish New Year is celebrated with foods such as apples and honey—symbols of wishing for a "sweet" new year.

Right, the Christian Church of Annunciation Opposite, in Israel, children are encouraged to begin reading sacred texts at a young age

People of the Christian faith also have several holy places in Israel. Many visit the Church of the Sepulchre, which is where Christians believe that the tomb of Jesus was found. Other people attend the Church of the Nativity in Bethlehem, the place that Christian believers call the birthplace of Jesus.

Throughout history, many religious wars have been fought in Israel. Even today, fighting still breaks out. That doesn't stop people from all over the world, and of different faiths, to come to Israel and visit holy **shrines**. Tourism has actually become big business for people running tours, hotels, and restaurants. While Israel has been divided by war, it still offers a peace and beauty like no other country in the world.

Glossary

Followers of **Christianity** believe in God as the sole deity and Jesus as his son and a prophet, or religious teacher.

When material is worn away from the earth's surface by weathering such as rain, flowing water, or wind, the process is called **erosion**.

Gorges are narrow passages through areas of land; a steep-walled canyon or part of a canyon is also known as a gorge.

A **habitat** is the environment where a plant or animal naturally lives and grows.

To **irrigate** crops, systems supply water to land that is dry; water can be pumped through long pipes from large wells or even rivers and lakes.

Judaism is the religion of Jewish people, or Judaists; they believe in God as the sole deity and follow many ceremonies and rituals set down in the Bible's Old Testament.

A **kosher** meal is one that is made up of foods approved by Jewish religious law and prepared following certain rituals.

People or animals that **migrate** travel from one location to another, usually because of changes in the seasons.

A **monument** is a stone or a building that is a reminder of someone important or an important event that happened.

A **Muslim**, a follower of **Islam**, or the Islamic religion, believes in Allah as the sole deity and Muhammad as his prophet, or religious teacher.

Areas in the country—out of the city—are known as **rural** lands; people who live in these country areas or small communities are said to be rural people.

A **savannah** is a treeless area of land that may contain bushes or grasses that grow well in a dry climate.

Shrines are places that are considered holy by religious people; visitors may come to pray and leave objects such as flowers or stones as signs of respect.

Tourism involves people traveling to places away from home for enjoyment or as learning experiences.

Index

alphabet, 23
animals, 13–15
army, 19
city life, 16, 19
climate, 10, 12
Dead Sea, 12

diamonds, 18
Dome of the Rock, 29
farming, 24, 26
flag, 9
food, 23–24
Golan Heights, 8
history, 4, 31

Jerusalem, 19–20
jobs, 17, 19
Jordan River, 6, 9, 29
landscape, 8
location, 7
National Water Carrier, 26

nature preserves, 15
Negev Desert, 8–9
plants, 13
population, 4, 16, 19
religion, 27, 29–30
rural life, 20, 22
savannah, 9

school, 16–17
Sea of Galilee, 22
size, 6, 13
tourism, 19, 31
wadis, 9